Real Facts About Bays

Branca Tani

Rosen REAL READERS

Rosen Classroom™
New York

This is a bay. It is a body of water that opens into a larger body of water.

Bays have many shapes.

Some are round.

Bays have land on three sides. The open side is where the bay meets a larger body of water. The opening is called the mouth of the bay.

This bay is next to an ocean.
Bays can also open into lakes.
They can also open into rivers.

The water in a bay
is usually calm.
This makes bays a good place
for boats to stop.

People swim in bays.

This family is swimming in a bay next to a lake.

Bays are a good place to fish.
The water is calmer
than an ocean, a lake, or a river.

Many types of animals live in bays. This boy caught a crab from a bay.

Some bays have harbors. This is where boats dock. These boats are docked in a harbor.

Some bays have ports.
Ports are where ships
pick up goods.
This ship is docked in a port.

Words to Know

bay

boat

crab

dock

land

ship